Collins Care for your

Goldfish

RSPCA PET GUIDE

Contents

New 3rd Edition
First published in 2004 by
Collins, an imprint of
HarperCollins*Publishers*
77-85 Fulham Palace Road
Hammersmith
London W6 8JB

The Collins website is www.collins.co.uk

Collins is a registered trademark of HarperCollins Publishers Limited

09 08 07 06
20 19 18 17

First published as *Care for your Goldfish* in 1980 by
William Collins Sons & Co Ltd, London

Second edition published in 1990

Reprinted in 1991 by HarperCollins*Publishers*
and subsequently reprinted 11 times

The RSPCA is a registered charity (no. 219099)
The RSPCA website is www.rspca.org.uk

Designed by: SP Creative Design
Editor: Heather Thomas
Design: Rolando Ugolini

Photographs and illustrations: Photomax UK: pages 25 and 40;
Acres Wild/Ian Smith: page 22; Acres Wild: pages 20–21

A catalogue record for this book is available from the British Library

ISBN-13 978 0 00 718272 5
ISBN-10 0 00 718272 4

Colour reproduction by Saxon Photolitho, Norfolk
Printed and bound by Printing Express Ltd, Hong Kong

Foreword

Owning goldfish is great fun but it is a responsibility. All animals need a regular routine and lots of attention. But, most importantly, pets need owners who are going to stay interested in them and committed to them all their lives.

Anyone who has ever enjoyed the company of a pet knows just how strong the bond can be. Children learn the meaning of loyalty, unselfishness and friendship by growing up with animals. Elderly or lonely people often depend on a pet for company and it has been proved that animals can help in the prevention of and recovery from physical or mental illness.

The decision to bring a pet into your home should always be discussed and agreed by everyone in the family. Bear in mind that parents are ultimately responsible for the health and well-being of the animal for the whole of its lifetime. If you are not prepared for the inevitable expense, time, patience and occasional frustration involved, then the RSPCA would much rather that you didn't have a pet.

Being responsible for a pet will completely change your life but if you make the decision to go ahead, think about offering a home to one of the thousands of animals in RSPCA animal centres throughout England and Wales. There are no animals more deserving of loving owners.

As for the care of your pet, this book should provide you with all the information you need to know to keep it happy and healthy for many years to come. Enjoy the experience!

Steve Cheetham MA, VetMB, MRCVS
Chief Veterinary Officer, RSPCA

Introduction

The goldfish, which was first bred by the Chinese over 4,500 years ago, was introduced into Britain in the early eighteenth century. It remains the most popular of all the coldwater fish that can be kept in captivity. Since fish are dependent on dissolved oxygen for their breathing, it is vitally important that steps are taken to ensure that oxygen replenishment of the water is both plentiful and continuous.

Goldfish bowls, in this respect, are too limited in size to be satisfactory, as their oxygen supply becomes depleted so rapidly. A rectangular aquarium with a reasonably large surface area should be regarded as the minimum criterion of accommodation for goldfish which, despite growing to quite a large size, have a relatively modest oxygen requirement.

Prize goldfish

Sometimes, goldfish are won at fêtes and fairs, and they are thus introduced to a family with no time for preparation. The practice of giving away live animals as prizes is not illegal, however distasteful it may be, but the mortality rate amongst such goldfish is high. In an attempt to be responsible, some stallholders may give the prize winners a small screw of paper which contains enough food to sustain a goldfish for the weekend. However, in the following 48 hours, it is more likely that the fish will die of suffocation or from sudden temperature fluctuations than starvation.

Those who accept goldfish as prizes should control their natural impulse to tip the new fish directly into a bigger container as soon as they get home. You should float the opened bag in the container for about 20 minutes until the two water temperatures are the same, then release the fish gently. Goldfish can accept a wide range of water temperatures but they must have time to acclimatize slowly; sudden changes of only a degree or so may be fatal.

Be prepared

Fortunately, most goldfish keepers, when deciding for themselves when they want to buy stock, will make adequate preparations in advance. Happily, it seems that there is always room for a pond, even in the smallest garden, and space for an aquarium, even in the most restricted accommodation.

The common goldfish

▲ Common goldfish

▼ Although the single-tailed Common Goldfish and the twin-tailed Lionhead are, scientifically speaking, identical species (*Carassius auratus auratus*), intensive breeding by aquarists has brought about the startling differences to their appearance.

Despite the tempting diversity found among the fancy varieties, the common goldfish, with its purity of line and extravagant colour, remains one of the most beautiful of all fish. The strong red-gold colour is always associated with the name, but many specimens are yellow-gold, and others show patches of silver or black.

For the novice fishkeeper, the common goldfish is the most suitable choice. The fancy varieties have been weakened, in some respects, by selective breeding which concentrates on certain characteristics of form and colour; the common goldfish retains the basic hardiness of the species.

Until they measure 12 cm (5 in) the common goldfish are suitable for keeping in an aquarium, together with similarly sized fish of the Comet, London Shubunkin and visibly scaled Fantail varieties. Over this size, all these would be too confined in a tank. They need the freedom of a garden pond, which they are hardy enough to tolerate all year round except in extreme climates.

In five years, the common goldfish may have reached a length of 20 cm (8 in) in favourable conditions; some fish will eventually attain 40 cm (16 in) in length and an age of some 25 years.

Fancy varieties

Single-tailed varieties

The first developments away from the common goldfish resulted in some interesting single-tailed varieties, with bigger caudal fins, and the existence of metallic (totally reflective), nacreous (semi-metallic) or matt (transparent) scales allowed other 'colours' to be seen.

The Comet

As befits its sleek looks, the Comet is capable of swimming very fast over short distances. The large caudal fin is often over half the body length again. Although plain yellow Comets are the most common, red-topped, white-bodied fish are becoming very popular. Comets may be kept out in a garden pond all year round; they often reach 14 years of age.

London and Bristol Shubunkins

Shubunkins are renowned for their incredible blue colour, mottled with black, red, brown, yellow and violet. London Shubunkins are, to all intents and purposes, coloured, non-metallic-scaled versions of the common goldfish. The heavy-lobed caudal fin and deeper body is typical of the Bristol Shubunkin. The London may overwinter in an outside pond but the Bristol is generally brought indoors.

▼ The colourful Bristol Shubunkin has a heavy-lobed caudal fin.

▲ The distinctive red-topped Sarasa Comet can be kept outside in a pond all year round.

Twin-tailed varieties

Despite their widely varying appearances, all the following fishes are varieties of the single species *Carassius auratus auratus*, the common goldfish. They have double anal and caudal fins, and are usually referred to collectively as twin-tails. Less hardy than single-tails, they are best kept in aquaria rather than ponds.

The Fantail

The Fantail has a spherical body, well-developed fins and a stiffly held, deeply divided tail. There are two types: a 'visibly scaled' variety with the normal metallic gold colouring; and a 'calico' variety with the colouring of a Shubunkin which is due to the lack of reflective material under the scales, giving them a 'scaleless' appearance. Only the metallic-coloured Fantail is hardy.

▲ The Moor's velvety black colouring makes an unusual contrast to the golden lines of its relatives. The telescope-eyes and flowing fins all add to its attractiveness.

▶ The divided caudal fin of the Veiltail hangs in distinctive folds, but these fins are easily damaged.

The Veiltail

This is another spherical variety, with the most excessive fin development. Unlike the Fantail, the Veiltail's divided caudal fin hangs in folds and the dorsal fin is very tall. The flowing fins are prone to damage and the Veiltails are best cared for in an aquarium where water conditions can be monitored and maintained at optimum quality much more easily than in a pond.

The Moor

Sometimes called the Telescopic-eyed Moor, this is a fish with the outline of a Veiltail. It should always be kept in an aquarium to safeguard the delicate fins and protuberant eyes. Some gold colour may be present but the best specimens are always entirely jet black; it is unnecessary to refer to this variety as the Black Moor.

▲ Adult Oranda showing typical head development.

The Pearlscale

The domed scales, each with a white centre, make the Pearlscale an easy fish to recognize. The body shape and fins are the same as those of the Fantail (opposite). Clean water conditions are essential to prevent the fins from becoming congested.

The Lionhead and Oranda

Both these fish have a bramble-like growth over the head. Lionheads are easily recognized – they have no dorsal fin.

◄ The Pearlscale is easy to recognize, as each dome-shaped scale has a white centre.

Biology

Temperature Goldfish are coldblooded or poikilothermic. Their body temperature is not stable, but fluctuates with the water temperature. Goldfish are able to tolerate the big range of temperatures they experience at different times of year in a garden pond because the variation is gradual. A sudden change of temperature, even if small, can be fatal. This is probably a significant factor in the high mortality rate of goldfish kept in captivity.

Eyes The bulbous eyes of the Telescopic-eyed Moor have been exaggerated by selective breeding, but all goldfish have slightly protuberant eyes. These compensate for the fish not being able to turn their heads. The result is a very wide field of vision, effectively enabling the fish to see all round. The eyes are entirely unprotected, with no eyelids. This is not a disadvantage to goldfish kept in a pond, but those in aquaria need to be shaded from direct sunshine.

Swim bladder The swim bladder is a gas-filled sac lying beneath the backbone. It acts as a buoyancy chamber, which prevents the goldfish from sinking when it stops swimming. It also causes the goldfish to float to the surface when it dies. The pressure within the swim bladder, regulating the density of the fish at varying depths, is adjusted by the secretion or absorption of gases from the blood.

▲ Telescopic-eyed Moor

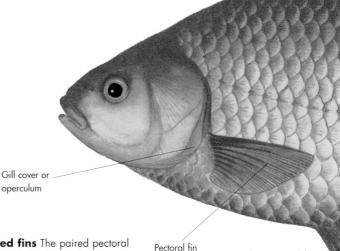

Gill cover or operculum

Pectoral fin

Pelvic or ventral fin

Gills All fish breathe by means of gills. These are internal organs where the exchange of gases takes place as a current of water is circulated through them. Dissolved oxygen from the water passes into the blood; carbon dioxide from the blood passes into the water. The water enters by way of the mouth, passes through the gills and out by way of the gill covers or opercula.

Paired fins The paired pectoral fins, just behind the gill opening, correspond to the fore limbs of land vertebrates. Their particular function is to act as brakes. A swimming goldfish will brake by extending both pectoral fins simultaneously. When extended, the drag they exert on the forward motion is sufficient to stop the fish. These fins are also used to change direction. By extending one, so that the drag is exerted on that side only, the fish can swing itself round to reverse its direction completely.

The paired pelvic fins correspond to the hind limbs of land vertebrates. To a lesser extent, these too are used in braking, but their function is to stabilize the fish by correcting the lift that occurs when the pectorals are used. Both sets of paired fins work like this, as hydroplanes, to control the rise and fall of the fish in the water.

Caudal fin The caudal, or tail, fin is used to help propel the fish through the water. The movements of the caudal fin are generated by the alternate contraction of strong muscles lying on each side of the backbone. These cause the sinuous swimming movement that passes like waves, down the length of the body from head to tail. Selective breeding from mutant forms has produced certain varieties of fancy goldfish, like the Comet, with vastly exaggerated tail fins.

Backbone The goldfish is a vertebrate, with a highly developed nervous system. The backbone is very flexible, adapted to bear the strain of the constant sinuous movements of swimming. Spines, corresponding to the rib bones of land vertebrates, are attached to the backbone, but they do not form a rib cage for the major organs. Instead these are contained in a membranous sac suspended from the backbone.

▲ Cutaway to show backbone

Scales The scales are thin, bony plates, overlapped from the head towards the tail for minimal resistance to the water, which form a complete, protective body covering. Each lays down extra growth rings with age, which can be seen under a microscope and interpreted by an experienced scale-reader.

▶ A scale

Colour The traditional metallic colour of the goldfish is due to reflective material (guanin) beneath the scales.

Dorsal fin

Caudal fin

Anal fin

Vent

Lateral line The lateral line is a major sense organ common to all fish. It is a line of specialized cells forming a fluid-filled canal, which makes the fish highly sensitive to the smallest disturbance of the water. Even very slight movement in the water will set up vibrations in this canal, alerting the goldfish to obstacles and to danger.

▲ Close-up of lateral line

Median fins The dorsal and anal fins are known, because of their position, as the median fins. Their structure is common to all the fins. Essentially they are folds of skin stretched over a light framework of fin rays. They are so fine that, in their median position, they are able to cut through the water with very little resistance, although some fast-swimming fish are able to fold down the dorsal fin when swimming at speed. The function of the median fins is to act as keels. By greatly increasing the longitudinal surface of the fish, they are able to give stability by preventing yawing and rolling.

Selecting goldfish

Which fish?

Despite the goldfish being a single species there is still a wide range of varieties you can choose from, so different is one type from another. Again, these differences in appearance give vital clues as to the fish's swimming habits, enabling you to select the correct fish for either indoor or outdoor cultivation.

Short stubby-bodied fish with long flowing fins are not to be found in nature – their inability to swim quickly would prevent them from escaping the attentions of any predator attracted by their bright colours; similarly, they would also find it difficult to chase for food. Such fish are best suited to life in indoor aquaria; after all, it would be a pity to banish their undeniable beauty and graceful movements to an outside garden pond.

Slim-bodied, short-finned fish are fast swimmers, more able to fend for themselves and look well either indoors or out. The fish conforming to this description are generally hardier, too, and are quite able to overwinter outside and to survive in icy conditions.

It is best to consider keeping related groups of varieties or to specialize in one particular type rather than keep a mixed community of all varieties, in which case, slower-moving fish will miss out at feeding times. Special care will need to be taken if breeding is to be undertaken, as keeping several types together will result in a likely loss of quality of young fish: successful breeders of high-quality fish always restrict their efforts to one or two varieties in order to maintain quality.

A good general guideline is to consider the hardy singletails as suitable fish for the aquarium or a pond all the year round, whereas the more delicate twin-tails should be

► Best considered as a pond fish, the Golden Orfe (*Idus idus*) is a surface-swimming fish.

kept mainly in well-maintained aquaria with occasional summer excursions, perhaps, to the outside pond. Of course, there are exceptions to this rule, and many metallic-scaled fantails may be able to survive the winter outdoors providing the pond is sufficiently deep to offer protection against ice.

Sources of fish

With the growing number of hypermarkets and garden centres, the fishkeeper is no longer tied to the traditional aquatic dealer for their livestock. One advantage of the modern garden centre is that you may well see the fish accommodated in typical ponds, together with associated plants, fountains and waterfalls, something that is difficult to visualize in a small shop, however well-stocked it may be.

Many local fishkeeping societies hold shows throughout the year, and there are several major shows each year where you can both see and buy suitable high-quality fish.

The monthly hobby magazines have plenty of advertisements (for plants and accessories as well as fish), or you may be lucky enough to find a fish breeder in your area who will be willing to part with some stock.

Picking healthy stock

Before actually selecting the fish you want, look around the shop first: it should be clean and well-maintained with stock clearly identified and priced. Tanks should not be overcrowded, nor have cloudy water. Fish should be swimming effortlessly, depending on variety: fish with long fins swim more slowly than short-finned varieties. Reject any with split fins, pimples, open sores, clamped-shut fins or concave, knife-edged bodies. Even if the fish you like appears totally healthy, do not buy it if it is in a tank with dead fish. A fish's colours should be dense and even; patchy, cloudy colours could spell trouble later on, if not with health then certainly in breeding, when the last thing you want is for such defects to be passed on to any young fish. If buying fish in an area away from home, ask the dealer about the water conditions to which the fish are accustomed.

► Fancy goldfish
including Orandas,
Bubble-eye and juvenile
Red-capped Lionheads.

Compatible fish

There are many other coldwater fish available, and some may be
regarded as possible tank or pond-mates for your goldfish. Many
North American fishes are very colourful but may be either too small
for the pond or may outgrow the aquarium.

Do not put wild-caught native fish in with goldfish; there is a real
risk of introducing disease and many require very well-oxygenated
conditions and thus may not last long in the aquarium. Tank-bred
specimens of bottom-dwelling tench may perform a scavenging
purpose in the pond but they will be hard to see unless they are of the
Golden variety. Golden Orfe are fast surface-swimming fish which love
to leap out of the water on summer days – they need a large pond if
they are to indulge themselves without ending up on the lawn! Resist
putting coldwater catfish in the pond; they can grow very large very
quickly and become predatory.

Aquaria

Fish tanks are usually of all-glass or single-piece plastic construction, but their size and surface area are the most important considerations. A small tank measuring 45 x 25 x 25 cm (18 x 10 x 10 in) would suffice as a quarantine or hospital treatment tank for a single fish, but a much better size for long-term fishkeeping would be 90 x 38 x 30 cm (36 x 15 x 12 in), holding 100 litres (22 gallons) and with a surface area of 2,700 sq cm (432 sq in). Note that fish tank dimensions are always expressed as length x height (depth) x width.

Fish capacity of tanks
To calculate a tank's fish-holding capacity, allow 1 cm of fish body length (excluding tail) per 60 sq cm of the tank's water surface area (1 in per 24 sq in). A tank of the dimensions suggested above would therefore be suitable for 45 cm (18 in) of fish: (90 x 30) ÷ 60 = 45 cm or (36 x 12) ÷ 24 = 18 in.

Surface area
Any fish tank needs a large surface area for good oxygenation of the water. A tall narrow tank may hold an equivalent amount of water, but the restricted surface area would greatly reduce its 'fish capacity', which is the number of fish that may be kept in the tank safely.

Aeration
The fish capacity of a tank is greatly increased by aeration, perhaps by as much as 40 per cent, but it is not necessary to aerate a tank for coldwater fish unless there is a danger of overcrowding or in very warm weather. A supply of compressed air from an air pump via a diffuser/airstone will create water turbulence and assist oxygen intake and carbon dioxide expellation at the surface. The air may be used to operate filters.

Heating and lighting
Goldfish need to be kept within the limits of 10–21°C (50–70°F). This is likely to be met in most living rooms throughout the year without a heater. Artificial lighting is not strictly necessary, but the aquarium plants should be provided with 8–10 hours of top lighting a day for the correct growth and photosynthesis. It will stimulate the fishes' activity and let you see into the tank. Fluorescent tubes provide more satisfactory lighting than tungsten bulbs as they emit less heat and have a longer working life.

► These Pearlscale Goldfish seem quite at ease in this well-planted aquarium. The clear space at the front of the tank means that the fish will always be swimming in full view.

Wiring

Water and electricity make bad partners, so any aquarium wiring should be done by a qualified person or under expert supervision. The use of waterproof fittings for the lights is recommended.

Position

The aquarium should be kept in a good north light but not on a window sill where it may be subjected to extremes of temperature or bright sunlight which causes overheating, oxygen loss and excessive algae growth.

Ventilated cover and cover-glass

A ventilated cover will keep dust off the surface of the water, allowing better oxygenation. It will also keep the fish safe from cats, and prevent them jumping out of the tank in fright at a sudden disturbance. A sheet of glass (or plastic equivalent) should be placed directly on the tank top before fitting the hood. This will cut down evaporation and protect the lamp fittings against damage from condensation and splashes.

Water

The domestic water supply is usually quite suitable for use in the aquarium, providing steps are taken to remove chlorine from it before use. This may be done by vigorous aeration for a few hours, or by the addition of dechlorinators which are available from an aquatic dealer.

Filters
Goldfish are foraging fishes, constantly stirring up sediment from the gravel. A filter will remove suspended matter from the water and keep it clear. Filters may be fitted either inside or outside the aquarium, and include box or canister types operated by air or electricity. Biological filters utilize natural bacteria to break down waste products; they are fitted out of sight under the gravel.

Gravel
Besides providing a medium in which the aquatic plants can root, the layer of gravel covering the base of the aquarium can also be utilized as a biological filter bed, in which bacteria can break down ammonia and other toxic waste compounds into safer materials.

Aquarium plants
A selection of submerged aquatic plants (see page 24) will provide food, shade and spawning sites for the fish, besides enhancing the look of the aquarium. They should be protected against being uprooted by foraging goldfish by placing some small pebbles around their base.

Shelter
Aquarium fish need shade from bright sunlight, and sheltering places. Hiding places can be provided by using rounded stones to form caves. Sharp-edged stones, or decorations, such as sea urchins, are potentially dangerous to the fish, which are liable to damage themselves on them. Any smooth, rounded rocks will need to be glued together with a silicone sealant to prevent them from toppling over.

Feeding ring
Goldfish will feed according to the temperature: probably twice a day in summer; once in winter. The use of a feeding ring prevents food floating over the surface of the tank and makes for easier cleaning.

Tank maintenance
Aquatic dealers sell scrapers for removing algae from the glass sides of the tank, and suction cleaners for siphoning off detritus, or decaying matter, from the base gravel. Regular partial water changes should be made every two to three weeks (see page 32).

Garden ponds

The garden pond is subjected to many more exterior forces than the indoor aquarium: wind and rain help keep the water 'moving' and free from stagnation; summer sun makes for healthy plant growth; and visiting insect or amphibious life supplement the food given by the fishkeeper.

Depth of water

If the garden pond is to be suitable for fish all year round, the water will need to be 45–60 cm (18–24 in) deep overall, with a shallow margin of 15 cm (6 in) where it will quickly warm up on an early summer day to encourage spawning. When, in severe weather, the surface water begins to ice over, the fish will congregate in the deepest part of the polythene-lined garden pond. Shallow ponds, which are subject to rapid fluctuations of temperature and are liable to freeze solid at times, should be used only as temporary summer ponds.

▼ This small garden pond, surrounded by paving stones, has been lined with polythene.

Excavation

When excavating for a pond, the depths stated opposite should be taken into account, making allowance for the fact that the water level will be lower than the surrounding ground level. The area of the pond needs to be big enough for its fringes to be planted with the rhizomes of water plants, such as yellow flag (see page 23), which need room to spread. Once excavated, the area should be lined with sifted soil, sand or newspapers, which act as an underlay for the pool liner. Without this, it is possible for the liner to be punctured by stones.

Pond liners

Of the many pond liners available, heavy-duty black polythene is effective and inexpensive, but only short-lived. Reinforced PVC or butyl are much more substantial and have the advantage that, if damaged, they can be patched. Pre-formed fibreglass pools are excellent, but they must be deep enough to give good shelter in winter.

Situation

Ponds are best sited away from overhanging trees. Falling leaves soon choke a pond and, unless raked out, will deplete the oxygen level in the water as they decompose. If leaves are unavoidable, then the pond may be netted in autumn.

How many fish?

Calculating a garden pond's fish-holding capacity may seem a little more complicated than for an indoor aquarium but a general (and very generous) guide is to allow 1 cm of fish body length per 10 litres of water (1 in per 5 gallons). If you have inherited a pond with your new home, the simplest way to calculate its volume is to multiply the surface area by the average depth to give the volume. (Measurements in centimetres divided by 1000 give litres; measurements in feet multiplied by 6.25 give Imperial gallons.) With irregular-shaped ponds, make a rough scale plan of the surface area using square paper before multiplying by the average depth. Of course, when the pond is drained and cleaned, you can measure how many bucketfuls it takes to empty it.

Autumn leaves

It is advisable to net the pond in autumn, to catch falling leaves that will otherwise choke the pond and use up its oxygen during their decomposition. If trapped under ice, fish may suffer serious oxygen starvation if there are decaying leaves depleting the oxygen level.

Algae

It is quite normal for newly set up, or re-stocked, ponds to turn bright green but they soon clear once the correct biological balance is established and the water plants are growing satisfactorily. Algae is best controlled naturally or by physical removal; any proprietary remedies may result in sudden massive 'algae-death' which can cause pollution problems.

Submerged plants

It is advisable to stock the newly set up pond with plenty of fast growing plants, such as *Elodea* or *Ceratophyllum* (see page 24). These will starve out undesirable algae by quickly consuming nutrients in the water. These two species need not be rooted as they absorb food through their leaves and stems directly, although weighting bunches of them down with strips of lead may make the pond look a little tidier.

Water lilies

Water lilies can be positioned in planting baskets anywhere in the pond. They provide valuable shade and shelter for the fish but may

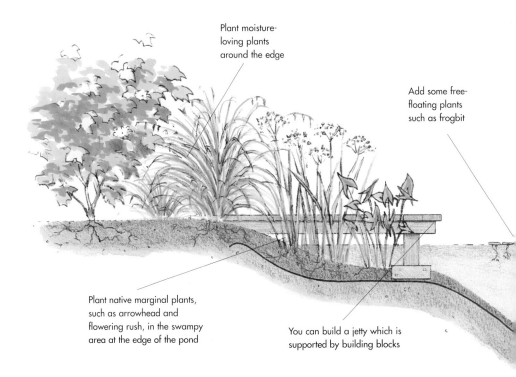

Plant moisture-loving plants around the edge

Add some free-floating plants such as frogbit

Plant native marginal plants, such as arrowhead and flowering rush, in the swampy area at the edge of the pond

You can build a jetty which is supported by building blocks

need lifting and pruning annually, in favourable conditions, to limit growth. Depending on species, water lilies need differing water depths: shallow water varieties planted in baskets should be placed on bricks so that their leaves just break the surface. Young specimens of deeper-water types are started off in a similar fashion but should be moved into increasing depths of water as they grow.

Planting baskets
Hessian-lined baskets filled with special aquarium compost, rather than garden soil, will prevent the root systems of vigorous-growing aquatic plants (such as water lilies) from over-running the pond. Baskets will make moving plants and cleaning out the pond easier, too.

Floating plants
Floating plants, such as *Azolla*, provide shade, shelter and food for the fish in the pond. They also inhibit the growth of algae in the summer months, by shading the surface.

Fountain
Even in a pond there may sometimes be a shortage of oxygen – for instance, in hot weather. A fountain or hose-pipe played on the pond at a critical time, such as when fish are seen to gulp at the surface, will

▼ A garden pond is the ideal accommodation for all hardy goldfish. There is room enough here for a small shoal of fish to live together, with adequate shade, shelter, depth of water – 45–60 cm (18–24 in) – and natural food.

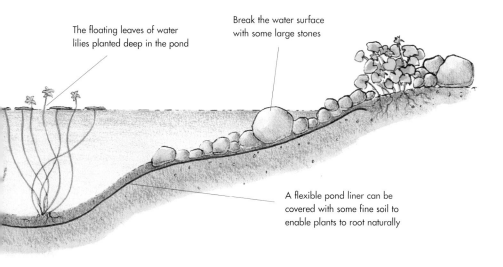

The floating leaves of water lilies planted deep in the pond

Break the water surface with some large stones

A flexible pond liner can be covered with some fine soil to enable plants to root naturally

▲ This attractive, well-stocked garden pond is surrounded by a variety of colourful water plants.

aerate the water temporarily. Water lilies will not tolerate water falling on them or vigorous water currents around them. The inlet supply to pumps driving fountains and waterfalls should be taken as near as possible to the returning water flow to minimize these adverse effects.

Pond surround

Paving stones placed around the edges of the pond not only provide a firm boundary but also help to hide the pond liner and protect PVC liners against the sun's damaging ultraviolet rays.

Lawn surround

A grass surround, which is likely to drain into the pond, should never be treated with chemicals, such as weed killers, that may also kill the fish.

Pond liner

It is important to protect the pond liner against damage from sharp stones. The excavated hole should be lined with a thick layer of sand or folded newspapers before placing the liner in position. Allow a wide margin of liner at the edge of the pond for tucking under paving stone surrounds.

Water plants

Emergent plants (suitable for ponds)

These are the marginal plants, such as arrow-head, marsh marigold, bulrush, water forget-me-not and yellow flag, which in nature grow at the water's edge, with the roots submerged and the leaves and flowers emerging above the surface. Besides adding to the beauty of the pond, the emergent plants, growing in a shallow margin, provide a spawning place for the adult goldfish and also some shelter for the young fry.

They can be planted in an artificial pond using a low wall to retain the soil, or in planting baskets. However, they all have stout, creeping rhizomes which, in favourable situations, need cutting back annually or they can become very invasive.

Floating-leaved plants (suitable for ponds)

Like the emergent plants, the best known of the floating-leaved plants, the water lily, has thick rhizomes which may also silt up the pond unless they are cut back when necessary. A specialist nursery will usually supply water lilies in planting baskets suitable for use in an artificial pond. As varieties of water lily grow to different heights, care must be taken to position the baskets at the correct depth so that the leaves will all lie on the surface.

Apart from their spectacular beauty, the water lilies, together with the other well-known floating-leaved plant, the ivy-leaved water crowfoot, provide sheltered resting places for the fish and, by shading the surface, inhibit the growth of algae.

▲ Arrow-head
Sagittaria sagittifolia
(emergent)

▲ Fairy moss
Azolla filiculoides
(floating)

▲ Water lily
Nymphaea spp.
(floating-leaved)

Floating plants (for ponds and aquaria)

These are small water plants which float freely on the surface, trailing fine, aquatic roots. The best known are duckweed and frogbit, which are able to take nutrients directly from the water by means of their roots. Although these plants provide food and shelter for the goldfish and inhibit the growth of algae, they multiply fast and can eventually cover the whole surface. For this reason, it may be better to introduce the less hardy *Azolla* or *Salvinia*. These are sub-tropical species which may possibly fail to overwinter in cooler climates, but they are the most suitable floating plants for an aquarium.

Submerged plants (for ponds and aquaria)

These are plants that are usually referred to as water weeds. They include Canadian pond weed, curly pond weed, eel grass, hornwort and water milfoil. They grow entirely under water and are particularly suited to aquaria where their beauty of form is best displayed.

Submerged plants feed through their stems and their finely divided or ribbon-shaped leaves. Their roots can be anchored in the gravel, perhaps weighted down by a stone or a small lead strip.

These plants are generally referred to as 'oxygenators', since they give off surplus oxygen in daylight (or under aquarium illumination) during their feeding process of photosynthesis. They also use up oxygen throughout the 24 hours for respiration, and thus a very heavily planted aquarium could become deficient in oxygen at night, especially during warm weather. Even so, the plants are valuable because they absorb carbon dioxide and use decomposing waste products – detritus – which are found on the floor of any aquarium as nutrients; this has the effect of purifying the water. These fast-growing plants will also inhibit the growth of algae.

▲ Water milfoil
Myriophyllum spicatum
(submerged)

▲ Curly pond weed
Potomageton crispus
(submerged)

▲ Hornwort
*Ceratophyllum
demersum* (submerged)

▲ Canadian pond weed
Elodea canadensis
(submerged)

◄ An aquarium that is well stocked with plants will look attractive as well as providing food, shade and spawning sites for the fish.

Submerged plants also provide shade and food for fish. Goldfish will eat the green plants directly, and also the minute organisms that are always found attached to these, as to all water plants. The most vigorous water plants will need some pruning, and small bundles of cuttings will root if they are anchored into the gravel at the base of an aquarium tank.

Rampant plants

Excessive pond plant growth cuts down swimming space for the fish and excludes light. The floating plant duckweed has already been mentioned in this respect, but emergent plants such as *Ranunculus*, submerged water lilies and *Elodea*, will also take over the pond completely unless they are restrained by pruning far-ranging roots and thinning over-vigorous growths.

Pond life

Once the pond becomes established (with all the things you have planned for it), nature simply adds to it. Birds will come to drink, insects will hover amongst the plants and amphibians will be regular visitors. It will seem that, however often you peer into its depths, there is always something new to see.

Amphibians

The massed jelly of frog spawn or the toads' strings are easy to see, but you will have to look more closely for newts' eggs. Each is individually wrapped in a water plant leaf. Not all types of tadpoles are eaten by the fish.

◀ Frog

▲ Newt

◀ Toad

Water insects

The fast-moving water skater uses surface tension to support itself as it hunts for drowning insects to eat.

Dragonflies lay eggs in the water, and the emerging larvae climb out on to a plant stem or leaf to extend and dry their wings before flying off gracefully.

Backswimming water boatmen are naturally buoyant, and they can only stay in place well below the water surface by hanging on to the submerged plants.

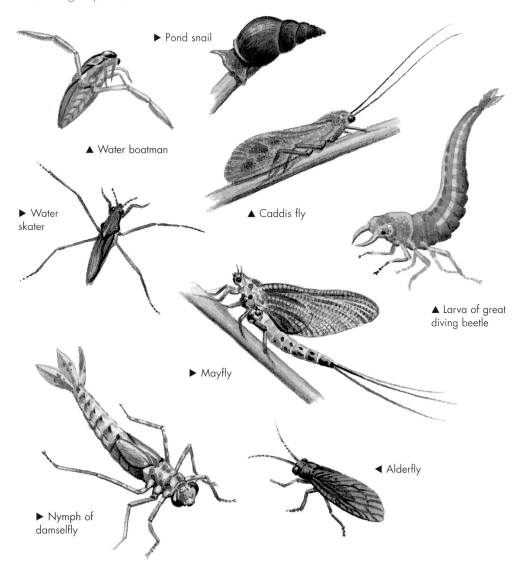

► Pond snail

▲ Water boatman

► Water skater

▲ Caddis fly

▲ Larva of great diving beetle

► Mayfly

◄ Alderfly

► Nymph of damselfly

Feeding

Goldfish in the aquarium

The rate at which goldfish feed is determined, like all their activity, by the temperature of their surroundings, on which, as cold-blooded animals, they are totally dependent. Outside the temperature range 10–21°C (50–70°F), the goldfish are too inactive to feed, either because of the cold or because warmer water is deficient in oxygen. With goldfish that are kept indoors in an aquarium, there will be less change in the water temperature and their feeding will be fairly constant all the year round.

Quantity of food

At indoor aquarium temperatures of 16–18°C (62–68°F), goldfish will require two or three meals a day. Each meal should be eaten in

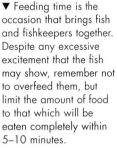

▼ Feeding time is the occasion that brings fish and fishkeepers together. Despite any excessive excitement that the fish may show, remember not to overfeed them, but limit the amount of food to that which will be eaten completely within 5–10 minutes.

Feeding ring

The use of a feeding ring is recommended, since it controls the spread of the food in the tank and makes cleaning much easier.

about 10 minutes and the amount given adjusted accordingly. Overfeeding leads to water pollution (not fatter fish) as uneaten food just sinks to the bottom to decay with the other detritus, using up precious oxygen in the process and fouling the water. It is very easy for different members of the family to feed the goldfish, unaware that someone else has already done so, therefore do make sure that everyone knows when the fish have just been fed.

Going on holiday?
Healthy, well-fed goldfish in a well-kept aquarium can last for up to two weeks without any food (see below). At holiday times, make sure that your fish are left in clean water with a good supply of water plants.

Goldfish food
In the aquarium, goldfish depend entirely on the fishkeeper for their food. Fortunately, proprietary brands of dried, flaked foods are very nutritious and specially formulated with the goldfish's dietary needs in mind. Always give 'goldfish food' rather than any other aquarium fish food. Goldfish should not be restricted to a single type of diet, however, and they will welcome some vegetable matter, such as chopped lettuce and spinach, rolled oats, etc.

While live aquatic crustaceans, such as water fleas (*Daphnia*), freshwater shrimps and water lice, may be relished along with *Tubifex*

Holiday care

Healthy, well-fed fish can generally be left to their own devices for up to two weeks. Giving a non-fishkeeping neighbour the task of feeding them may result in over-feeding unless small pre-packed 'meals' are left, with *very* strict instructions on how to feed them. Alternatively, you can purchase a 'vacation feeder', which releases small food particles over a period of time. However, a responsible person should be asked to check the tank daily to ensure that electrical equipment is working properly.

worms, there is always a risk of the introduction of disease with these 'wild-caught' waterborne animals. Many fishkeepers may prefer to offer frozen, or freeze-dried, versions of these foods instead. Non-aquatic worm foods are also greedily accepted by goldfish: chopped garden worms or cultured white-worms will help to bring out the very best condition in the fish.

Goldfish in the pond

Although to us, early spring sunshine appears welcomingly warm, it takes a great amount of steady sunshine to raise a garden pond's water temperature from the chill of winter. It is not until the water temperature remains constantly over 10°C (50°F) that the fish emerge from their state of winter torpidity and begin feeding. Adding food to the pond before this time will only add to the decaying matter on the pond floor.

Quantity of food

One of the advantages a pond fish has over its indoor counterpart is that it receives a much more varied diet. Along with insects and their larvae, minute aquatic animals all find their way into the pond and, together with soft-leaved pond plants, make up an incalculable part of the fishes' food intake. When evaluating the amount and frequency of food to be given, the golden rule is 'little and often': no more than will be eaten in a few minutes. Once the fish appear disinterested (or even spit the food out), then too much food has been given. Remember that it is very difficult to see uneaten food at the bottom of a pond, so err on the miserly side at all times.

Seasonal variations

Pond fish will feed regularly throughout the warm summer months and then their appetites appear to increase as autumn comes. This is an

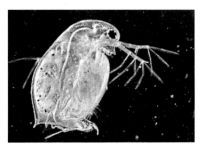

▲ Water flea (*Daphnia*)

▲ Freshwater shrimp (*Gammarus sp.*)

instinctive measure on the part of the fish in order to lay down reserves of fat to see them through the winter months when they feed little and are almost immobile. Care should be taken to ensure that a good supply of nutritious foods is given at this time, when natural foods in the pond may be on the decline.

Proprietary foods
Long-floating proprietary foods are especially suitable for pond fish and are available in pellet or 'stick' forms. One advantage of these foods is that by remaining on the surface for long periods, they provide you with more time to see the fish at close range, in addition to allowing you to evaluate just how long the fish take to eat. These two jobs are made more difficult in a pond where there is no glass panel through which to observe underwater proceedings.

Wild food
Again, the fishes' menu may be expanded to include some wild-caught aquatic live foods with the proviso that all such foods may be carriers of disease and should also be screened to exclude dangerous waterborne insect larvae (see page 38), or cleaned thoroughly in running water (especially *Tubifex* worms) before being given to the fish.

Other food
Some fish appear to take pieces of cheese, cooked potatoes, bread and biscuits, etc. However, it might be wise to test such foods on aquarium fish first, in order to observe that they actually eat the food and that it does not pass rapidly through the system and emerge undigested to pollute the water. In any event, no greasy, highly-spiced or fatty foods should ever be offered to either pond or aquarium fish.

▲ Water lice (*Asellus sp.*)

▲ Mass of *Tubifex* worms

Maintenance

One of the main advantages of fishkeeping is that it demands relatively short periods of effort on the pet owner's part to keep things running smoothly. A few minutes a day, an hour or two a month, is all that is required – although you can expect to spend much more time than that once you include fish-watching!

Aquarium maintenance

The most important task (apart from counting the fish at feeding times) is to carry out regular partial water changes; this keeps the level of dissolved wastes down to a minimum.

- Remove 10–20 per cent every two to three weeks (siphoning water from the bottom of the aquarium removes some detritus, too) and then replace with some fresh, previously dechlorinated water which is of approximately the same temperature.
- Remove any dead leaves from plants, and prune and take cuttings from the rapidly-growing species.
- Remove algae from the front glass panel of the aqarium with an algae scraper; growths on the rear and side walls can be left.
- Clean the cover-glass so that the plants receive the optimum amount of light. Be sure to replace fluorescent tubes at least once a year.
- Clean the filter medium (foam inserts or aquarium filter 'wool') by rinsing in *aquarium water* and then replace it; renew if it is very dirty or has had repeated uses.

▶ Scraping algae off the front glass panel of the aquarium with a plastic algae scraper tool.

Pond maintenance

Apart from removing fallen leaves and thinning out water plants where necessary, outdoor ponds will need cleaning out periodically; this is best done before the winter or otherwise in early spring.

● You should start off by removing all the decaying vegetation and any accumulation of mud.

● You must take out most of the water first in order to make catching the fish easier, and do not forget to search the muddy bottom for any fish that may have sought refuge there.

● Keep the fish in a large container of pond water while the pond is being cleaned – a paddling pool is ideal for this but always cover it to protect the fish from any cats! If possible, allow a few days to elapse before you re-introduce the fish to the pond in order that the new water may become fully dechlorinated.

● Before putting new plants in the pond (or while they are removed during cleaning), inspect them for snails' eggs and larval stages of other aquatic creatures which should be removed. Trim water lily root stocks if necessary and then replant them in baskets.

● Clean the fountain or waterfall pump filters and inspect cascades and other external watercourses for any leaks or obstructions.

● Any external pond filters can be backflushed periodically in order to clean them, but you should always follow the manufacturer's instructions closely in this respect.

● Finally, you should always make sure that you check the condition of the pond-cover and your special anti-ice equipment before winter comes. Don't leave it too late; prevention is always the best policy.

◀ Blanketweed will soon choke pond plants if it is not removed promptly. A stick twisted around in the water will prove to be the most efficient method of removing excessive growth although smaller quantities can usually be combed out by hand without harming the plants. Do not bother to untangle blanketweed from fast-growing plants such as *Elodea* or *Ceratophyllum* – any plants lost with removed blanketweed will soon be replaced quite naturally.

Protecting your fish

Aquaria

Although with an indoor aquarium you have total control over its conditions, there are some external factors that may upset the equilibrium.

Water temperature

This will fluctuate naturally during any 24-hour period, varying more quickly in smaller tanks. Site the aquarium away from direct sunshine to prevent overheating especially in summer; if necessary, shade the tank with a cloth. If water temperatures rise very high, maintain the oxygen levels in the water by extra aeration. Float a sealed plastic bag of ice cubes in the tank to lower the temperature quickly only in extreme cases.

Air pollutants

Paint fumes and tobacco will enter the water through the aerator. Turn it off if you have to use any strong polish or disinfectant near the aquarium.

Wild-caught live food

Beware of inadvertently introducing disease or harmful animals into your aquarium through unclean food (see page 31).

▶ It is well worth making the effort to protect and maintain your fishes' environment when they can present you with such a rewarding picture. Notice how a dark-coloured liner shows up the fish more attractively.

Ponds

The outdoor garden pond has its own share of risks, some of which are natural and some man-made. Take precautions as outlined below.

Netting a pond

When netting a pond to protect your fish from predators, remember to leave access for other pond residents, such as frogs and toads. Peg the net down securely but allow it to rise slightly over edging rocks or stones.

Ice

Providing the pond has sufficient depth (at least 45 cm (18 in) to prevent solid freezing, there will be an area of relatively warmer water at the bottom of the pond where the fish can survive safely during the winter. There may be a risk that toxic gases produced by decaying vegetation will build up under the ice, so the ice covering should be ventilated or partially removed. Pond covers may prevent icing entirely but lowering the water level slightly, coupled with the use of floating heaters and floating anti-ice devices, will help to maintain openings in the pond to allow air to circulate over the water surface. *Never* open up the ice with hammer blows.

Other risks

You should guard against leaves falling from any nearby trees and weedkillers blowing or draining into the pond.

Predators and parasites

Pondfish fall victim to herons and cats which can be discouraged by netting, low trip-wires or floating guards. However, there are also less obvious predators in the pond itself: dragonfly and great diving beetle larvae also kill young goldfish.

Newly hatched goldfish fry are also at risk from *Hydra*, a freshwater coelenterate, which stuns its prey with a paralyzing sting, and from *Cyclops*, often introduced with water fleas as food.

Anchorworm (*Lernaea*) and the fish louse (*Argulus*) attach themselves to a fish's skin and burrow into the tissue beneath, whilst *Dactylogyrus*, *Gyrodactylus* and *Ergasilus* direct their parasitic attentions to the fish's gills.

Snail populations, which are often introduced into a garden pond via bird droppings or on new water plants, may soon grow to epidemic proportions unless they are checked.

Handling your fish

Fish are highly sensitive creatures, which are easily hurt by careless handling and easily shocked by sudden changes in temperature or light and by strong vibrations.

When you are moving fish to temporary accommodation, it is very important that you protect them from injury by using a net or a jug to catch them. If you use your hands, then it is likely that some scales will be torn off, allowing *Saprolegnia* (see page 38) to enter. Once this fungus spreads to the gill covers, it can cause interference with the fishes' breathing and subsequent death.

Temporary accommodation for the fish needs to be prepared long enough in advance for the temperature to be within 1°C (2°F) of the permanent accommodation at that time. The shock of a sudden change of temperature which is greater than this is sufficient sometimes to kill a fish.

Be aware that it is also dangerous to plunge fish from sudden light into darkness, or vice versa. In an aquarium that is lit by a fluorescent tube, the light should be turned off before the room lights at night in order to make the transition to darkness more gradual for the fish.

Fish are also shocked by sudden noise and vibration, such as tapping on the side of the tank. They will die after being stranded out of water, having jumped out in fright. This is one reason for always having a ventilated lid fitted on the aquarium.

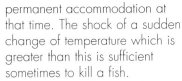

◄ Netting fish is a stressful time for fish and fishkeeper alike. Using a large net (or two) will make the job easier.

The healthy goldfish

In general, goldfish are hardy and healthy, and their distressingly high mortality rate is more often due to poor living conditions, wrong feeding, bad handling, foul water, injury, pests or sudden temperature fluctuation than to disease.

A sick fish should always be isolated in a separate tank, and if the cause of its loss of condition has been due to its poor living accommodation, this move alone may effect a cure.

A new fish should also be kept in isolation for a period in order to ensure that disease is not transmitted to the existing stock.

Signs of health

Abdomen	It should be well-rounded, neither hollow, nor distended, except in females carrying eggs.
Appetite	It should be good in well-oxygenated water on warm days. Appetite is much diminished in cold water and in warm water low in oxygen.
Breathing	A rhythmical rise and fall of the gill covers indicates normal breathing. Gulping at the surface is a sign of oxygen starvation.
Demeanour	The fish should be alert to stimuli, active in warm water, although activity is much reduced in cold water, or when oxygen is low. Gregarious: one fish leaving the shoal to lurk alone may be in deteriorating health.
Eyes	They should be bright and clear.
Fins	They should be intact, without tears, splits, white spot or streaks of blood. Fins should be held away from the body. Drooping and folded fins are a symptom of ill health.
Position in water	A fish should be freely swimming on an even keel. Sick fish may sink to the bottom or float on the surface on their side.
Scales	These are covered with an invisible mucus, which is a protective body covering while it remains unbroken. Scales should show no injury or fungal growth.
Vent	It should be clean, free of faeces, which do not trail from a healthy fish.

Ailments

Oxygen starvation

Gaping at the surface may be due to lack of oxygen in the water, or the fish's inability to make use of what oxygen is present through infestation of the gills by parasites. Swift investigation and remedial action is necessary.

Oxygen starvation can happen in a pond as a result of overcrowding, decomposing vegetation, shallow water (which tends to overheat on a hot day) or blanketweed choking the surface. The oxygen level of the water can quickly be improved by playing a fountain, or a hosepipe on the surface.

In an aquarium, add vigorous aeration and siphon out excess detritus from the aquarium floor, replacing any water removed in the process with fresh, at approximately the same temperature. If the fish's gills are held wide and are inflamed then a parasitic attack is more likely to be the cause than poor water conditions. Subsequently it is vital to correct the reasons for poor oxygenation, taking the advice of a professional aquarist or a veterinary surgeon, if the reason is more obscure.

▲ *Saprolegnia* or fungus disease

Fungus disease, *Saprolegnia*

This is a common and very contagious disease among goldfish which results in many deaths. The spores of the fungus, *Saprolegnia*, are often present in ponds and aquaria but can gain entry to the fish only through wounds. The body and fins are covered in white tufts, but similar growths around the mouth (so-called 'Mouth Fungus') may be due to an entirely different organism, requiring antibiotic treatment instead of the usual anti-fungal remedies.

Lightly affected fish can be treated in the aquarium but heavily infested fish and pondfish should be treated in an isolation tank. An alternative isolation treatment is the salt bath – a three per cent saline solution daily for 15–20 minutes (but remove fish sooner if distress is shown). Sulphonamide drugs, which are available on veterinary prescription, may be needed for advanced cases.

Constipation

Trailing faeces are an indication of constipation, which often results from feeding goldfish exclusively on dried food. A more varied diet, including vegetable matter and some live food such as *Daphnia*, together with the use of medicated food, should effect a cure.

White spot disease, *Ichthyophthiriasis*

Another common, contagious and often fatal ailment of fish is white spot disease, caused by a parasite and characterized by tiny white spots all over the skin, fins and gills. These should not be confused with the spots found on the gill covers of male fish at breeding time.

Modern, easily obtainable remedies enable fish to be treated without removing them from the aquarium or pond, but manufacturers' instructions must be closely followed as overdosing, just to be 'on the safe side', often proves to be just the opposite. As most remedies colour the water, the amount of light reaching the plants will be reduced and some finer-leaved plants may suffer a temporary setback.

Fin rot

Accidental tears and splits to the fishes' fins heal of their own accord, but fin rot is the wasting of the tissue between the fin rays. Although proprietary remedies and the salt bath treatment (see fungus disease, opposite) may prove effective, fin rot is considered to be the result of poor feeding and substandard aquarium conditions. Attention to rectifying these errors will not only bring about a lasting cure but will also prevent further outbreaks of fin rot.

Dropsy

An extremely bloated body and standing-out scales are indicative of this condition. It is better to destroy the fish humanely than attempt a cure.

Swim bladder disease

Loss of balance is the most obvious, although non-specific, symptom of swim bladder disease, which is common among goldfish, and particularly so among the highly bred fancy varieties. Although there is no known cure for the disease, the condition is sometimes relieved by keeping the affected fish in shallow water for a few days and giving it a salt bath treatment (see fungus disease, opposite).

▲ Fin rot

▲ *Ichthyophthiriasis* or white spot

Reproduction

Maintaining quality

All goldfish, regardless of variety, are the same species and will interbreed without hesitation. Fishbreeders take advantage of this, by deliberately putting together two fish, which are chosen for their best features, to produce high-quality offspring. However, allowing random, unplanned breeding will produce poor-quality young – a waste of resources and effort. It is better to breed quality rather than quantity.

Sexing goldfish

▼ These goldfish are spawning. The breeding season lasts from spring throughout the summer.

Even fish biologists make no claim to being able to sex a goldfish on sight, except those in breeding condition. Then the female will show an abdomen swollen by an ovary full of eggs, which is the hard roe, and the male will produce enough sperm, or milt, in the soft roe to fertilize the eggs of many females. The males also have white tubercles on the gill covers at this time, and on the pectoral fins which may look enlarged.

Breeding season

The breeding season begins as the weather warms up and continues throughout the summer. Mature fish which are over one year old and in breeding condition are capable of spawning approximately monthly during the breeding season.

Breeding condition

The breeding condition can be encouraged by good feeding in the spring. The goldfish will need a high-protein diet with plenty of fresh food, such as water fleas and scraped meat. An increased diet will allow them to produce eggs and milt as well as normal growth. Goldfish will not usually breed in water that is not clean and well oxygenated.

Breeding in a pond

Goldfish have been known to breed in temperatures ranging from 10–21°C (50–70°F), but the perfect day for the first spawning is a warm, still day in early summer. A shallow pond margin, where the water will quickly warm through, is ideal and will encourage breeding, as also will the presence of water weeds or bundles of willow twigs which can be put there specially to receive the eggs as they are laid.

Spawning

Spawning behaviour is noisy and unmistakable. The males chase the females through the pond into the shallows, with much splashing and commotion, causing them to release batches of eggs over any available water plants or substitutes. The males release milt over the eggs, thereby fertilizing them. Spawning frequently begins early in the morning and may continue all day.

The eggs

The eggs, which are the size of pin heads and look like clear jelly, float singly through the water in their thousands and, being sticky, adhere to whatever plant they were released over. The eggs and the young fry are in danger of being eaten by adult fish in the pond. For safety, they should either be removed, still attached to their support, to a hatching tank or netted off from the main area of water. The warmer water of the shallows, if partitioned off, makes an ideal natural hatchery.

Breeding in an aquarium

Aquarium breeding is more suitable for a pair of fish than for many. You will need a well-fitting glass partition for two reasons: first, to separate the adults for a few days, so that when it is removed they are encouraged to spawn; and then to separate them from the eggs.

Hatchery tanks

A hatching tank may be used for the eggs that are laid in either a pond or an aquarium. It should be filled with fresh tap water, and left to stand for a few hours, before introducing the eggs with the plants to which they are attached. A sunny window sill will be a suitable position to maintain the water at 21°C (70°F). However, strong sunshine falling directly on the water surface is too intense for the goldfish fry. Duckweed may be floated on the surface of the water to provide shade, while the temperature remains high enough to encourage good growth.

▲ These fish eggs are adhering to pond weed.

The young

Hatching

The eggs will hatch within four to fourteen days, according to temperature. Ideally, in a temperature of 21°C (70°F), they will hatch in four days, whereas at 10°C (50°F) hatching will take fourteen days, and during all that time the eggs are in danger from water snails, insect larvae and adult goldfish.

The young fry

When they first emerge, the young fry look like fine hairs and continue to hang from the plants. In a few days, when they are free-swimming, they will have absorbed their own yolk-sacs and they will need a proprietary food specially prepared for fry. Those kept in a pond will also be able to feed naturally on microscopic animal life.

In nature, thousands of eggs are laid, but only a few fish reach maturity; in captivity, it may be that too many are being raised in a confined space. It should be remembered that the fish capacity of a tank is very limited, and it has been calculated that to rear 1,000 fry to a length of 2.5 cm (1 in), you would need 84 tanks measuring 60 x 30 x 30 cm (24 x 12 x 12 in).

Feeding the fry

At one month, the goldfish fry can begin to make the transition to an adult diet; at three months, hardy breeds may be put out into a garden pond. These are dull in colour, and the full glory of their adult gold may take up to a year to develop.

Summary

Breeding goldfish is not difficult, the urge to reproduce being a very strong instinct even among animals kept in captivity. In order that your fish produce strong, healthy young, all you need to do is put into practice the guidance given in this book. Whether indoors or out, you should always keep your fish under the very best of conditions at all times and they will do the rest for you!

▶ A group of young
Lionhead goldfish.

Your questions answered

We shall be moving house soon and want to take our fish with us. What's the best (and easiest) way of managing this?

Transport your fish in the largest container you can manage, especially if the journey is to be a long one. Clean plastic 'dustbins' are ideal and their clip-on lids stop the water slopping about too much. A suitable alternative is to beg or borrow a polystyrene box from a fish shop; these are excellent on two counts – they act as insulated containers (keeping the fish cool in summer) and are also watertight (remember to tape the lid on). Never overcrowd or overfill the container, and use a battery-operated air pump during warm weather if necessary. Take as much of the fish's aquarium water with you as you can, to lessen the shock of their new water conditions, and they must be acclimatized accordingly. Plants can be transported in layers of very wet newspapers; gravel can be left in the aquarium but take out rocks that otherwise might topple and break the glass during transit.

How can I stop my pond going green?

Because a garden pond needs to be in sunshine, there will always be a risk of the water turning green, especially just after cleaning out. This is due to the nutrient-rich water on the one hand and not enough aquatic plants to compete with the algae on the other. Make sure that there are always plenty of fast-growing 'oxygenating' plants in the pond. Although algae removers may kill the algae quite effectively, large amounts of algae suddenly dying often pollutes the pond further. External filters can help to keep the water clear as well as remove visible and invisible waste products.

My dealer says a goldfish bowl isn't satisfactory accommodation. Why is this?

Fill a goldfish bowl with water and watch what happens: once you pass the halfway stage the water surface area decreases as more water is put in. Although this gives the fish more room to swim, there is less chance for oxygen to be replaced. Anyway, would you want to swim around in circles all the time?

Is is true that goldfish eat ants' eggs?

Yes and no! Goldfish will eat ants' eggs but these are no longer considered to be a goldfish's staple diet. Proprietary, specially formulated foods are far better and the supply is more dependable.

My pond plants are becoming smothered with algae. Can it be cleared?

The best way to deal with blanketweed is to remove it physically by twirling a stick amongst it to collect it like a stick of green candy-floss. Shading part of the surface of the pond with water lilies may also help lessen the risk of blanketweed forming.

How can I stop cats or herons getting at the fish?

Tripwires of black threads −15 cm (6 in) off the ground − around or across the pond may deter herons but be otherwise inconvenient or unsightly. A life-size replica of a heron standing at the pond may also help to put off real birds. Floating plastic imitation 'lilypads' will not support the weight of a cat's paw, and one or two soakings usually teach the cat the obvious moral.

My goldfish are chasing each other. Why?

This is usually the best sign you can have to prove that everything in the pond or aquarium is in tip-top condition! The fish are mating; usually the male chases the female into warmer, shallower water or into thick clumps of aquatic plants where eggs are scattered and fertilized.

I think my pond's leaking, how can I trace the leak and mend it?

▲ These fantails are swimming among the plants in an aquarium.

If your pond has a fountain, make sure all the water falls back into the pond; obviously in windy conditions some water will be blown elsewhere. Similarly, cascade watercourses should be checked for obstructions which can lead to unnoticed overflows. Otherwise, the only real answer is to drain off the pond and look for cracks (in concrete ponds) or for splits or tears in the liner. Frost damage may cause the former while tree roots can easily cause the latter. Patching kits allow easy repair in liner ponds. Concrete ponds are more difficult and 'lining' these is one answer.

Life history

Scientific name	*Carassius auratus auratus*
Name of young	Fry
Eggs hatch	4–14 days
No. of eggs shed	1,000–3,000
Fertilization	External
Puberty	8–12 months
Adult coloration	8–12 months
Best age to breed	2⅓ years
Spawning season	April–September
Spawning cycle	Monthly
Length at 5 years	20 cm (8 in) in common goldfish
Adult length	40 cm (16 in) in common goldfish
Life expectancy	25 years (common goldfish) 14 years (fancy varieties)

Index

Why not learn more about other popular pets with further titles from the bestselling RSPCA Pet Guide series?

PET GUIDE

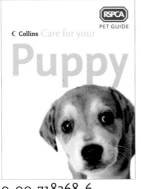

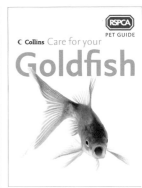

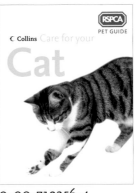

To order any of these titles, please telephone **0870 787 1732**

For further information about all Collins books, visit our website: **www.collins.co.uk**